origins

origins

For those bored with the shallow end

Simon Parke

A Crossroad Book
The Crossroad Publishing Company
New York

First published in Great Britain in 2001
Azure
1 Marylebone Road
London NW1 4DU

First published in the United States of America in 2001
The Crossroad Publishing Company
481 Eighth Avenue, Suite 1550, New York, NY 10001

Printed in the United States of America

Library of Congress Cataloging-in-Publication Data

Parke, Simon.
    Origins : for those bored with the shallow end / Simon Parke.
      p. cm.
    ISBN 0-8245-1910-8
    I. Title.
    PR6116.A74 O74 2001
    821'.92 – dc21

                               2001001426

1 2 3 4 5 6 7 8 9 10   06 05 04 03 02 01

To Joy
40 and fab

WELL DONE

This morning I'm drawing from a well.
I'm lowering the bucket.
It's a familiar well.
I've drawn from it often.
And the rope used to be long enough.
But these days,
I'm not so sure.
I seem to get less water every time.

Until, last Thursday, I got none.
Nothing at all.
A little bit the day after.
But it looks like nothing again today.

I'm beginning to wonder
if I might need to move on.
I don't want to.

But what served me once
is serving me no longer.

Clearly all is not well.

PLATE AGAIN

The plate holding my sausages.
Looks solid.
But that, as we know, is an illusion.
For every supposed solid is nothing but
a loose and shifting gathering of molecules;
and every molecule,
a riot of a million fast and furious atoms.
And every atom?
Every atom a resonating hum
of string-like musical energy.

So the plate holding my sausage.
It's no plate at all really.
But a billion symphony orchestras.
And they're dancing as they play.

Is anything as it seems?

WILLY WISE OWL

What is the wisest thing ever said?
Certainly in the Top Ten
are the following three words:

Make no assumptions.

Because our capacity to misread a situation,
or simply to be wrong,
is as infinite as the Milky Way.

DESERT WARM

As any desert dweller will tell you,
when looking for firewood among the big sands —
and you will need to,
for it's very cold at night —
you should look *beneath* the sand.
Where the wicked wind has buried it.

Dig down.
Just because you don't see it
on the surface,
doesn't mean it isn't there.

If you want to keep warm amid the cold,
dig down.

WOULD YOU ADAM AND EVE IT?

What happened in the Garden of Eden
was that Eve and Adam
lost their sense of openness
toward God.

After the apple incident,
things suddenly got more furtive,
more hidden.
And I'm not just talking fig leaves.

So when God turned up looking for them,
asking how they were,
to Eve and Adam
it felt like a problem,
an invasion.
A nosy neighbor
rather than a well-loved friend.

I'd quite like to get back to the friendship.

11

A GENIAL QUESTION

So the genie pops out of the bottle
and asks the question.
You're surprised—and not a little frightened.
Because the question—it may be dangerous:
What would you desire
if there was no praise—
and no blame?

If there were no circumstances to limit,
no watching eyes to condemn,
no mealy mouths to "tut, tut,"
no adoring public to appease,
no praise, no blame:
What would you desire?

In other words,
who is the real you?

12

WE NEVER MET

The playwright Terence Rattigan
never could acknowledge his homosexuality.
The stiff upper lip mentality
made his deepest longings
a matter of repressed deception.
He lived a polished, but significant, dishonesty.

Graham Greene said that
talking to him was
"like walking on very slippery parquet flooring."

The origin of a genuine encounter?
Two people meeting
unafraid of what's inside them.

CONSENTING ADULTS

Authority.
Where does it come from?
A uniform?
Police, priest—
that sort of thing?
No. And thrice no.

So where does it come from?
A role?
Parent, teacher, political leader—
that sort of thing?
Hardly. Not nowadays. Sorry.

God?
Nice try.
But most people wouldn't recognize God
if he, or indeed she, sat on their laps.

No. Authority comes from you.
It comes from you giving your consent to someone.

Please consent carefully.

BURST HOPES

Tears at the graveside.
Unsurprising in itself.
But it wasn't a traditional burial.
There was no coffin for instance.
Or indeed a body.
Just a burst balloon,
being laid to rest,
in a solemn garden ceremony.

Stupid of course.
But not for the child.
For him, it's all that matters right now.

And through his eyes,
if the adults aren't able to take this loss seriously,
then how can they be trusted with anything else?

*The origin of being a good parent
is being able to bury,
with due reverence,
a stretchy piece of rubber.*

HOW BECOMING

Everyone needs a soul friend.
One who offers you
the big and liberating possibility of being understood;
one with whom there is space to stretch out,
and be known;
one with whom the masks are slowly taken off
and the half-truths discarded.

Entering the deepest temple of your spirit,
they help you discover the mystery of
who you have been,
who you are,
and what you might become.

A soul friend.
I'd love one of those.

16

ORIGINAL. AND WORST.

Humpty Dumpty sat on the wall.
Humpty Dumpty had a great fall.
All the king's horses
and all the king's men
couldn't put Humpty together again.

But perhaps that's just as well, really.
Because maybe some light
can now shine through Humpty's cracks.
Shine in.
Shine out.

Humpty. He's cursing his luck.
But the truth is:
sometimes the original isn't best.

AN INCIDENTAL MATTER

He does 51 push-ups every morning.
He does 51 because of Psalm 51.
It's a prayer in the Bible for forgiveness.

When he has finished his push-ups,
he says, with racing heart,
"Lord have mercy."
And he knows it is so.
So off he goes to work,
and during the day that develops,
he tries to forgive earth for not being heaven.

The origin of a forgiving spirit
is being forgiven.
The origin of a merciful spirit
is the experience of mercy.

And the push-ups?
Well, frankly, they're slightly incidental.

FAMILY VALUES

You'll have heard people say,
"She's like a sister to me,"
or, "He was like a second father as I grew up."

As if we can invent our own families!
"This one isn't working —
let's make one that does."
Oh, so it's Do-It-Yourself families now, is it?
I mean, what's the world coming to?

Its senses.

As Jesus hung on the cross,
he looked at his mother
and his friend John, and said:
John — this is now your mother.
Mary — this is now your son."

The true origin of family lies
in our need of support and care
in the difficult business of living.

Family is not primarily about blood.
But about being there for people.

VIRTUE REALITY

Amid the torrential spoiling rain within
and the jerky gusts of wind,
in the darkest undergrowth of my sodden soul,
I was surprised to find a candle burning.
It was not one I had lit.
Or even protected.
It was just one I discovered.

It was God's home sign.
God's house light.
And the beginning of virtue in me.

20

NATURE PROGRAMMED

A stream is nature.
A canal is culture.

A grunt is nature.
Language is culture.

Competition is nature.
Sport is culture.

Sex is nature.
Marriage is culture.

Wild flowers are nature.
Manicured lawns are culture.

Nature is raw.
Culture is cooked, seasoned,
chopped, presented.

Nature is you.
Culture is fancy dress.
And not to be worn too seriously.

EARLY LEARNING

Hitler told his secretary
that during one of the many beatings
his father gave him,
he managed to stop himself from crying,
to feel nothing —
and even to count the 32 strokes received.

He learned early in life to deny the pain,
and his feelings of rage and powerlessness
against this man,
to deny the absence of mercy.

An inspiring tale indeed.

Except for the ending.

22

CHURCH

Originally, what?
A building?
No.
An institution?
No.

*Church: a loose association of the crippled,
hobbling in, or toward, the mercy pool—
and seeing what happens.*

Ahh! *The original.* And best.

DAMN

We'd talked about the flood.
The possibility of it. How we'd handle it.
Wise things to do in the emergency.
But the discussion — it was all a little hypothetical,
and a little "dry."
And so when the dam did eventually burst,
and the water smashed through us,
all our talk meant very little.

We went with the flow, as they say.
And so did our homes.
Some drowned.
The lucky clung to tree roots,
and staggered back to tell the tale.

The scouts say: Be prepared.
The prophets say: Be wise.
But when life is fired at point blank range,
it can all count for nothing.

24

THE REAL THING

So the teenager likes Coca-Cola.
Are we surprised?
There's a *Star Wars* video on his desk,
a large quantity of computer magazines.
Oh, and he's training to be the new Buddha
for the five million members of the Kagyu sect.

The boy god is also keen on the Spice Girls.
And finds Tibetan music "really quite boring."
He eats Tibetan dumplings.
But he prefers the two-day-old Hawaiian pizzas
flown in occasionally by supporters in New Delhi.

"My faith comes and goes," he says,
"and sometimes it's hard when people come to see me —
it is difficult to know what to say."

Endearing honesty.
And a quiet reminder that religious leaders
aren't very different from the rest of us.

25

JEALOUS GUY

I watch Miranda.
Today, she is with Sue.

Tomorrow, she's going round to Steve's
for a meal.

Last week, she was with Errol, Joy, and Mel
at her office party.

I am jealous of Sue, Steve, Errol, Joy, and Mel.
Because I want to acquire Miranda.
I want to have her for myself.

The origin of jealousy is acquisitiveness.
The outcome of jealousy
is anything from ache and bitterness
to maiming and murder.

THE STRAWBERRY

You'll know the story.
You're being chased by a tiger.
You get to the edge of the cliff.
You grab a vine and begin to shin down a rock face.

Suddenly you realize there is another tiger
waiting for you at the bottom.
And there's a mouse chewing at the vine.

Caught between these two monsters,
you realize you are face to face
with a strawberry growing on the cliff face.
You eat it.
You enjoy it.
It is the best strawberry you have ever tasted.

*The origin of happiness is to be able
to live the moment.*

AFTER THE STRAWBERRY

With the strawberry eaten,
the vine breaks, and you fall toward the tiger,
hating the mouse, cursing the mouse.

If the mouse hadn't chewed,
you wouldn't be ogling tiger teeth
and about to die.

And then the tiger's gone!
Suddenly runs off.
Why?

A noise.
And the answer.
The mouse. It has fallen too.
And frightened the tiger. Tigers hate mice.

That which had destroyed you — the mouse —
now comes to save you.
Indeed it was the only thing that could.

Without the mouse, you'd still be hanging safe,
but hopeless, between the two tigers.

The curse is blessed.

CONDUCT UNBECOMING

The church organist has the dog put down.
Conduct unbecoming.

The vicar has the organist moved on.
Conduct unbecoming.

The bishop has the vicar sacked.
Conduct unbecoming.

The archbishop has the bishop resign.
Conduct unbecoming.

God has the archbishop removed.
Conduct unbecoming.

The dog has God retire early.
Conduct unbecoming.

When it comes to judgment,
everyone's got a case.

IT'S ABOUT TIME

The Egyptians were responsible for the first calendars.
They calculated that the moon rose 12 times,
between each flooding of the Nile,
when they could sow their crops.
So an annual cycle of 12 moonths —
or months — was established.

Denys the Little, monk and astronomer
in what is now South-west Russia,
reset the calendar to work from the birth of Christ
rather than the reign of the emperor Diocletian.
So 248 Anno Diocletiani became Anno Domini 532.
And suddenly Denys lived in the 6th century!

Julius Caesar, of course, had introduced the Leap Year,
which was further tinkered with
in the Gregorian calendar of 1582
(named after Pope Gregory).

Britain adopted the Gregorian calendar in 1752,
when 2 September was followed by 14 September.
Just like that! We still use it.

Time. How will you use it today?

THE WHEEL THING

This elderly couple.
We often meet in the street.
And one day he's pushing her in the wheelchair.
And the next day, she's pushing him.
They alternate.

Know what?
I reckon they're having a relationship.

THE OLD SAUCEPAN

The origin of litter can be traced
to a small Bronze Age man called Ogrith
who was angry with God
and wanted to trash his garden —
which of course is the world.

So he flung his broken Bronze Age saucepan
into the forest and said "Good riddance."

Since then, descendants of Ogrith,
whether spiritual or actual,
have further lost touch with their creator.
And of course when awe and reverence go,
so does respect for the environment.

And so the bus ticket is dropped on the sidewalk.
The potato chip bag flung out of the car window.
And untreated shit pumped into the sea.

Whose garden is it anyway?

PLANE TRUTH

Jesus.
Carpenter.
Wood work.
If you'd let him.

YOU MUST COME ROUND!

The first recorded yawn
in the history of the human race
is well documented
and occurred in that uncomfortable millennium,
before fire was discovered,
when wheels were still square,
and Nelf grunted to her neighbor Crod:

"You really must come by
and look at the wall paintings of our vacation.
We've just got them back."

*One of the endearing things about the human race
is that whatever staggering technological advances we make,
we really don't change as people.*

So a few millennia later,
for Nelf, Crod, and wall painting
read Chloe, Jim, and camcorder.
But the yawn is the same.

And it's massive.

FENCE OR FLOWER?

Their friends and family are fighting
to save their marriage.

What they should be doing
is fighting to save their friendship.

Friendship is bigger, more holy,
more ultimate, than marriage.

Protect the flower.
Not the fence around it.

35

A TRAVEL AGENT

In one sense, it will be
the plane that takes her to Thailand.
Of course.
But in another sense,
it will be the tears.

The tears she cried
when her husband died,
and she declared her world to be over.

Now, a year later, I meet her in the street,
and she tells me of her travel plans.
"It's a time for a new adventure," she says.
"Thailand, then probably America.
And a friend in Canada says I must drop in."

The plane will carry her.
Brilliant.
But it was the tears that made
the whole adventure possible.

WAIT FOR IT!

The origin of patience
lies in detaching myself
from the desire to control.
It's as simple and impossible as that.

Patience.
You've waited long enough.

AN AUTHORITATIVE STATEMENT

The origin of true authority
is being able to say sorry.

When the man,
for the first time in his life,
said sorry to his 12-year-old daughter,
he thought civilization as we know it might crumble.

From here on,
they'd both know that he made
quite as many mistakes as she did.
There was no way back from here.
It felt like the end of his authority.

In fact, it proved to be the beginning.

*She now felt he might just turn out to be
a half-decent dad.*

LANCELOT

They say that a lot of hate and judgment in us
comes from projection.
We project onto others
what we don't like in ourselves.

We don't consciously do it.
It's more an unwitting act of survival.
It gives us a break from ourselves.
After all, who wants to face their own darkness?

But imagine one day the courtroom drama
taking a surprising turn.
I'm prosecuting as usual,
and doing a very good job,
when suddenly I realize
that I am also the defendant.
I'm prosecuting myself.
Oh no!

Oh yes.
I'm condemned by my own lips.
But it's strange what a deep sense of peace
can follow this shocking discovery.

Something of a lanced boil really.
From here on, Lancelot.

DO AS I SAY?

The word "obedience"
has negative overtones for most of us.
Examples of hideous obedience
stain the paths of history.
Obedience that has crippled,
enslaved, tortured, murdered.
It feels like a distant word. A cold word.
A strong figure imposing his will on someone else.

But the origin of the word "obedience"
is something slightly different.
It's from the Latin word "audire,"
which means to listen.
And listening is a close word. A warm word.

If I am obedient to you, I listen to you.
Simple as that.

*What I do with my listening
rather depends on what you say.*

FIRST, THE END

Sometimes the end comes at the beginning.
Sometimes it's all completely back to front,
and we have the outcome before the origin.

You have a fear of heights?
A fear of flying?
Then do a parachute jump.

Why not? It's only a fear.
It's not real.

Jump first.
And ask *why* you didn't want to later.

Sometimes the answer lies in doing,
the outcome before seeking the origin
Because sometimes the beginning comes at the end.

TOO OBVIOUS

Although a writer may hate
some of the characters she creates,
in the end she must love them.
In order for them to live and breathe.

And although a director may despair
of some of the cast he's working with,
in the end he must love them.
In order for them to flower and flourish.

And although God may ache sometimes at—

You're there ahead of me.

OUT OF HIS MIND?

Do you think God was out of his mind
when he created us?
It is, after all, such a *risk* creating things.
Particularly things like me,
with all the reliability of a bus timetable.

God must have been out of his mind.

No.
Not out of his mind.
Out of his love.
That's where we came from.
Where you came from.
Out of his love.
And you'll return there too.

Nice.

QUESTION TIME

The scientist asks how it works.
The painter asks how it looks.
The counselor asks how it feels.
The mystic asks where it came from.
And they all need each other.

CONCENTRATE, RUDOLF!

How could someone come to be
commandant of a concentration camp?
Would that person have to be especially evil?

Rudolf Hoess, commandant at Auschwitz, said this:
"Above all, I was constantly reminded that
I was to comply with, and follow,
the wishes and commands of parents,
teachers, priests. . . . Whatever they said, went."

Don't you love an obedient child?

OLD SAND

It's said that the Namib desert
is the loneliest, most unchanging,
most infinite place on earth.
It's also reckoned to be
the oldest desert on the planet.
The original.

Its essence is the drifting red dunes, soaring and bare,
crossed only by the most courageous of animals
like the oryx gazelle or the sandviper.

The isolated tracks they leave only heighten
the overwhelming sense of solitude.
They do not find company in their journeying.

But they do survive.

Know how they feel?

46

THE TRUTH MARKET

Surprisingly, you don't generally find the truth
at the truth-sellers market.
Just a mass of confident voices
all in loud and competitive disagreement.

So you journey home, disappointed.
Get lost on the way.
And trip over something,
small but hard.

Further inspection reveals it to be a bit of the truth!
Your cursing stops.
Your heart sings.
And you hold it close.

It's not the whole truth.
But it'll do for the moment.

God things come to those who wait . . .

ONLY JOKING!

According to Jesus,
good persons bring good
out of the treasure of good things in their heart;
and bad persons bring bad
out of their inner storehouse of bad.
For the mouth speaks what the heart is full of.

Thus, the origin of the words we speak,
is the person we are within. Oops!

So the next time someone says,
"Only joking!"
or, "Must have been the drink talking!"
take pity on that person, by all means.

But don't believe.

MIST OPPORTUNITIES

The story has been that the origin of the word "Posh"
could be found on the suitcase labels of the rich,
as they travelled to India by boat.

"Portside Out, Starboard Home."
(Abbreviated to POSH.)
This would give them the cool side both ways
amid the excessive heat
of the Indian Ocean.

Sadly, this story turns out to be untrue.
More likely, "Posh" was slang for "Dandy."
But we're not sure.
The truth, as so often,
is lost in the mists of time.

Mists of time.
Nice phrase.
Couldn't find its origin.
Lost in itself, apparently . . .

SAY R

So I want to be humble.
In the library, I look under "H."
"Humility — and how I achieved it."
Interesting.
Under "F"?
"Five humble men — and how I trained the other four."
Fine.

I want to be humble,
but I'm looking in the wrong place.
I should be looking under "R."

R for Reality.
Humility is the gift of the realists,
who know they have much to be humble about.

See what you lack, not what you have.
Say "R."

That is the root of humility.

DON'T TOUCH

When you flirted with me,
touched me,
seduced me,
kissed me,
you led me to believe things about myself
that I'd never dared believe.

Now I discover it isn't so.
Not as I imagined.
Gently, you tell me the truth. So gently.
You just want to be friends.

The seeds of shame, need, insecurity—
they lay so long inside me.
Undared, unfulfilled, unpublic longings.
Humiliation is their exposure to myself.
To you. To others.

And that is never gentle.
Not gentle at all . . .

51

LOSING THE PLOT

Our new TV.
32-inch screen.
Surround sound.
Cable. Digital. Satellite.
We have the gear.
State of the audio-visual art.
Cutting-edge stuff.
Fantastic!

The programs are still crap, though . . .

In the end, all the TV has is its program.
And in the end—
putting aside your reputation—
all you have is your story.

How's it going?

DARK THOUGHTS

Darkness.
It is the nest of the soul.
We are released from the prison of required shape,
where we need be this, that, or the other;
we are relieved of the strain of being exposed.

Darkness.
It is the nest of the soul,
as the call to function dies away,
the pressure to perform dissipates,
the requirement to impress fades.

I crawl into the shelter of the night,
the obscurity of the deep shade,
the hidden cover of the furrow,
the warmth of the womb,
for this darkness —
it is the nest of my soul.

LIGHTEN UP!

Light.
It's the origin of life.

Imagine.
If the sun were to turn its gaze
and look away awhile —
and we become the shadowland.
A shadowland of dying
where no human, animal, or plant survives.

Warmth goes cold.
Color is starved at source.
And the slow chill of planet freeze begins.

shadow
grey
chill
dark
freeze
death

Pray that tomorrow
the deep curtain-drawn dark before the dawn
once again gives way to the tugging fingers of light.

HEAD ON HEART

Most fundamentalism can be
traced back to a sad divorce —
the divorce of ideas and affection,
intellect and friendship,
head and heart.
As if one could live without the other . . .

The loving thought.
The thoughtful feeling.
The compassionate mind.
The caring intellect.
Here is the proper unity.
United they stand, and divided — we all fall.

Fundamentalism is the offspring of the divorce.
It is a sick little bastard
who grows up to speak guilt and fear.
But not homecoming.

Can't speak of what you haven't experienced.

FOOLISH

Passion —
can't help itself.
It really can't.

It ignores all warnings.
Tramples on moral beliefs.
Grips.
Grows.
And then it destroys.

Passion.
It's the foolishness of humans.
It's also, strangely enough,
the foolishness of God.

THE PROPOSAL

Johnny Hide was an agent
who helped Marilyn Monroe
during a particularly bleak time in her career.
He was, of course, infatuated.
Offered her a million dollars to marry him.
In the end, knowing he had only months to live,
he encouraged her to marry him anyway
if only to secure his inheritance.
She was poor. It was tempting.
But she turned him down:

"The person I wanted to help most in my life
— Johnny Hide —
remained someone for whom I could do almost nothing.
He needed something I didn't have — love.
And love is something you can't invent,
no matter how much you want to."

But if you can't invent it —
even for a million dollars —
where does it come from?

I'M FINE!

If I let my anger out,
it would pull the whole world down, he said.

If I began to cry now,
I don't think I'd ever stop, she said.

How are you? I asked.
Can't complain, she replied with a smile.
Well, you can, she added —
but it won't do much good!

True.
She has multiple sclerosis.

The things we're asked to carry around
within our little skin and bone . . .

THE FROG WHO DIDN'T LEAP

Drop a frog in hot water
and it will leap out.
Place a frog in warm water,
heat slowly, and it will stay there —
and be boiled to death.

Gradual changes in climate aren't noticed.
But they can be lethal.

So the 6-year-old boy
shoots the 6-year-old girl in America.
No surprise.
Amid the gradual grip of gun climate.

It is the unnoticed struggle.
The unreported war.
And yet the battle for climate —
in individual soul, institution, office, or nation —
it's the biggest battle of all.

KNITTING

Imagine if sex were for
the knitting together of souls
amid this cold and crying cosmos.

*And also enjoy just seeing sex and knitting
appear in the same sentence.*

JESUS IS A FAT MAN

Jesus is a fat man with a mobile phone.
I know. Because I saw him.
He got out of the bus,
slightly breathless,
helped the old lady out,
and walked her slowly toward her front door.
She fumbled for her keys, with shaking hands
which once were young, but now were old;
which once attracted, but now repelled.
"See you tomorrow, Maud," said the fat man.
"See you tomorrow, love."

If it wasn't Jesus,
it was someone very like him.

THE FAILURE OF FEAR

The hungry schoolchildren
looked longingly through the baker's window.
All those cakes! And doughnuts!

But teacher said they mustn't be hungry.
And teacher frightened them.
So they weren't hungry.
Not at all.
Their stomachs rumbled.
The sweet smell of fresh baked bread hurt.
And their imaginations ran amok with iced buns.
But they weren't hungry!
Oh no!

Fear.
It can make you pretend things.
But it can't help you change things.

MURDER MOST FOUL?

The pain of Charles Darwin
was that he didn't want to say what he saw.

He didn't want "to murder God."
Or upset his friends in Victorian society.
Or disturb his devout wife.

And so he waited twenty years to
publish his theory of natural selection,
which suggested that humans could be the result
of development through evolution,
as other species clearly were.

Until then, of course,
humans were perceived to be
the direct creation of God,
as described in the Genesis stories.

"The subject haunted me," Darwin wrote later.
Keeping it to himself probably made him ill.
He published in the end because
another scientist threatened to be the first.
Hence, *On the Origin of Species.*

Reports of God's murder were, however, premature.
Truth isn't murder. Truth is life.

EXPLAINING IT AWAY

So the joke is that the woman
he met in the elevator turns out to be
the same one he later meets in the bakery,
only this time the policeman is drunk
and mistakes her dog for the hippo
who previously had knocked over the vase
with the cold tea in it —
the one that had caused the stain in the first place,
only of course no one knew that
until the woman's uncle
gave her umbrella to the boy,
who then recognized that the car
didn't belong to the mayor at all.
Or rather it did,
but not how they imagined!
If you see what I mean . . .

Do you get it now?

*An explained joke has never been
the origin of a good laugh.*

64

CALLED TO THE BAR?

Last night he noticed that there was
something wrong with the beer.
Not as it should be.
He took it back.
Suggested the barman check the barrel.

Tonight, though, the beer was perfect.
He didn't give it a thought.
Just drank.

The origin of the pain inside you —
that's worth tracing back.
Because the evening won't get started until you do.

But the origin of the joy inside you —
don't trace that back.

Just dance.

THAT'S A BIG CHOICE!

Some people can only see
one side of the argument.
They tend to be bigots.

Some people can see
both sides of the argument.
They tend to be uninvolved.

Some people *live* both sides of the argument.
They tend to get crucified.

The choice is yours.

DIAMOND GEEZER

It was his fortieth birthday.
He was asked what he had learned
over the years.
He wasn't sure he had learned very much.
He was sad right now.
Things were difficult with his family.
But he did know that once
he had touched the diamond.
That once, at a particular time,
and for a brief moment,
everything had come together.

And he knew that before he died
he would like to touch the diamond again.

THE ART OF TRUTH

The art historian was getting angry.
There was an irritating man in his tour party.

The art historian wanted to talk
about the *form* of the painting.
The irritating man kept asking about its *meaning*.

The art historian considered the *Baptism of Christ*
and pointed out the interesting use of light —
a technique used by a number
of subsequent Italian artists.
The irritating man, however, just wanted
to ask about how Jesus must have felt
at this defining moment in his life.

The art historian talked choice of paint.
The irritating man talked choice of paths:
the moment when each of us
becomes aware of our destiny,
aware of our relationship
to ourselves and the world.

For the art historian, this was a job.
For the irritating man, this was
a brush with the truth.

A MUSICAL SCORE

It was disgusting!
That's what people said when the news broke.

After all, she was his piano teacher.
And he was seven years younger than she was.
Many felt she had abused her role
when it was discovered that
they had had sex.
On more than one occasion!
His parents were furious.

God, however, was more forgiving.
After all, they were only young.

And frankly, what does anyone really know
at the tender ages of 69 and 62 respectively?

BACON FOILED

The mad pig leaps over the cliff.
I catch it. I save it — and then wish it well,
in its fresh start,
down here on the beach.
It grunts thanks,
breathes in the new air,
takes a huge and succulent
mouthful of seaweed,
runs headlong into the sea.
And drowns.

The beach.
It could have been a good place for the pig.
But not until he'd asked
what brought him here.
Not until he'd found out
why he jumped off the cliff.
What it was that drove him mad in the first place.

There's more to fresh starts
than the feel of new sand between your trotters.

NOUGHT FOR YOUR COMFORT

You'd think that a zero
was fairly basic to things.
The sort of thing a civilization
would organize pretty soon after discovering fire
and inventing the wheel.

Not so.
It was only in 1202 that
the zero finally got a firm foothold in Europe.

For two centuries prior to this,
the system of numerals that included the zero
had been toyed with by the Christian church —
but rejected as part of the number system
of the Arab "infidel," who had picked it up
from Hindu number-crunchers.

But truth is truth. Wherever it comes from.
And by the 16th century,
the zero had transformed the art
of European calculation.

And of course, at last, the scoring feats
of our football team could be accurately recorded.

LOVE CHILD

The children of Mahatma Gandhi were many.
Scandal?
No salvation.

His strategy of nonviolence spawned many spiritual heirs
around the world.

So here's to the Dalai Lama in Tibet;
Rosa Parks and Martin Luther King in the U.S.A;
Lech Walesa in Poland;
Aung San Suu Kyi in Myanmar;
Benigno Aquino Jr. in the Philippines;
Desmond Tutu and Nelson Mandela in South Africa.

Mahatma means Great Soul.
Great Souls have great children.

Whose child are you?
And will you have children of your own?

SOUNDS OF SILENCE

There are different sorts of silence.

The silence of admiration. Awe — better than applause.

The silence of contempt — not even
bothering to respond.

The silence of fear — you could say something,
but you are frightened.

The silence of the broken heart — deep wounds
beyond the sad cycle of recrimination and rebuke.

The silence of contemplation — a pondering, listening stillness.

The silence of tragedy — the scene surveyed so
bleak that all words are stupid.

The silence of mutual trust — sometimes company
is best enjoyed wordless.

And the silence before the beginning of the world?
What sort of a silence was that?

NICE

The origin of being nice?
It's having nothing left to defend:
no barricades of fear, prejudice, or arrogance.

It's having no rights to protect.
No territory to be threatened.
It's having died already,
and risen beyond the small arrows
fired by frustrated lives.

It's having lain so broken
that there is nothing left inside you
that can be hurt.

Leaving within only the loving recognition
of hurt in others.

It's surprisingly costly.
But nice.

THE PLACE

There is a place within us all,
that is too painful to go to.

It is hard to find, thankfully.
Well-protected.
Most experiences in life
don't take us anywhere near there.

The paths to it are secret.
Its existence unacknowledged.

This place.
It is the center of our emotions.

It's not the part
that makes us cry at slightly sad films.
Rather, it is the place within
that, when reached, destroys us.
Ruthlessly protected,
but once the defenses are breached,
a place of infinite softness, vulnerability and pain.

God help you if you have to go there.

75

BEYOND COMPASS

This moment.
As I look at you.
And you look at me—
what's it worth?
Passing pleasure.
Or lasting treasure?

Friends joined as clinging clay
before the start of time.
And at last you've found me.
And I've found you.
And we can cling together again.

Yet I still fear the cold call
of the unformed tomorrow.
And no compass invented to guide me.
To guide me beyond this moment.

*Growing up is learning to live lovingly
without such a compass.*

THREE CRADLES

Archaeologists discover three cradles
in the Middle East.
Those of baby Mohammed,
baby Jesus,
and baby Abraham.
How sweet.

And didn't they all do well?
Those who have founded major world religions
are quite an exclusive club.

But sadly, as the three families gather round the cradles,
an argument starts, and a fight breaks out.
Not quite sure who started it,
but it seems some people were feeling insecure.

Must have been that.
Because difference divides only the insecure.
Difference feeds the holy.

IN ALL CONSCIENCE

We are agreed.
Whatever seed of conscience
exists in the newborn baby,
it is significantly shaped and watered
by parental attitudes.

The small child takes good note
of what they regard as good behavior
and bad.

But that isn't the whole story.

After all, those who throughout history
have shown the greatest ethical insight
have been rebels against the standards around them.
Something inside tells them No.
How so?

It seems the healthy conscience
outgrows its surroundings.
Its true origins lie elsewhere.

Mystery.

CAMERA. LIGHTS. ACTION!

"Mary had a little lamb,
its fleece as white as snow.
And everywhere that Mary went
the little lamb would go."

It was a man with a high-pitched voice
who recited the poem.
And surprisingly, among the group who listened,
there wasn't a child in sight.
But what happened next
was more surprising still.
For the strange contraption on the desk
then played back to them
the poem they had just heard.
Amazing.
The phonograph was born.

The man with the high-pitched voice
also of course invented the movie camera
and the light bulb.

Thomas Edison.
1847–1931.
He invented a lot of the 20th century, really.

79

STUPID WOMAN

The stupid woman!
She may be in a state of shock,
but I'm afraid she's still stupid.
The terrible news story has broken.
And now she's dribbling on about
how surprised she is that such
a thing could happen in her village.

After all, it wasn't the city.
They were a close-knit community.
She thought she knew everyone.
Evil happened somewhere else.
In bad places.
Where there weren't nice lawns
and nice gardens.

Excuse me, but the Garden of Eden
is said to have had some cracking herbaceous borders.
Didn't save them.

ORIGIN OBSCURE

How did you get inside my soul?
How did you come to inhabit it
quite so fully?
Through which door did you come?
It was as if you knew the way.
Instinctively.

And now you're there.
For good or ill.
Gift. Pain.
But something inside so strong.

I don't know how you did it.
I just feel the force.

WILL POWER

The slings and arrows of outrageous fortune.

My salad days when I was green in judgment.

Shall I compare thee to a summer's day?

Now is the winter of our discontent.

The unkindest cut of all.

A tale told by an idiot, full of sound and fury,
signifying nothing.

Star-cross'd lovers.

William Shakespeare.
We know nothing about his inner life.
But a thousand words and phrases
into which we can pour our hopes and dreams
is a better knowing really.

The weary sun hath made a golden set
And, by the bright tract of his fiery car,
Gives token of a goodly day tomorrow.

Sleep well.

WHO NEEDS IT?

I don't think God particularly
needs my confession.
He forgave me long ago.
Maybe even before I was born.

But I do think that *I* need my confession.
To break down the feelings of defensiveness
that build up inside me
like limescale in a kettle.

The limescale flakes its way into my tea.
The defensiveness flakes its way into my relationships.

Neither improves the taste.

CENTER HOLD

When the center cannot hold,
mere anarchy is loosed upon the world.

And if I am to survive today,
my center will need to be strong:
strong to cope with the pull of opposites within.

The urge to dominate,
the urge to submit.
To turn outward to others,
to hide in my shell.
To aspire to the spiritual,
to grasp the physical.
To give the kindly word,
to scream and act my pain.

The pendulum swings within,
the terrible ebb and flow,
and if the center cannot hold, what then?

A harsh splintering, deep dislocation,
and the broken wreck of a life
I once hoped to sail safely
into a distant port at my journey's end.

If my center cannot hold.
If my center cannot be held —

I don't know, but maybe this is a prayer.

BRIGHT IDEAS

Right, so let me just check
I've heard you right, madam:
that's one diving suit,
one parachute,
one telescope,
some automatic doors,
the robot,
an automatic assault weapon,
scissors various,
and the folding furniture.
Well, that all seems in order.

Oh, and the tank.
Mustn't forget madam's tank, must we?

All the above were, of course,
the inventions of Leonardo da Vinci.

And the *Mona Lisa* — of *course,* madam.
Where would you like Gordon to put that?
No need to be rude, madam.
Gordon's doing his best . . .

DAY TO DAY

Addicts.
People dealing with their pain.
But not necessarily dealing with it very well.

Well, I'm not anyway.
Though I suppose like everyone,
I have good and bad days.

Yesterday went quite well.
Today?
Ask me tomorrow.

Addicts like me live from day to day.

A RUNAWAY VICTORY

Early in the marathon,
I put competitor 342 well behind me.
Goodbye sucker!
Unfortunately, by the end of the marathon
competitor 342 had put me well behind him.
Hello sucker!

Too often, what people call *letting go,*
is in fact *running away.*
And what we run from
has a nasty habit of catching up with us.

The root of letting go
is not letting go.
But making friends
with the offending feeling or situation.

Or at least speak your pain to it.
Enter into some sort of conversation.
Possible?

It may beat attempts at a runaway victory.

AS A RULE

The origin of the fence
had been to protect the beautiful flower.
However, after a while,
the fence became so overgrown,
that the flower was hidden from sight.
The fence was promptly ripped down.
So a happy ending there.

Oh. And as soon as a rule
becomes more important
than the good it was meant to protect —
that should be ripped down too.

Choose your good.
Then choose your rules to protect it.

But remember: only your good will get to heaven.
Rules, apparently, don't fit through the gates.

END TIMES

Suicide.
Is despair at the root?
Or is it often more about anger?

You are dropped by your girlfriend.
Sacked by your boss.
Denied by your parents.
Mistreated by prison officers.

You decide to make a point.
Explain this away!
So there you are, dangling on a rope;
or, mortuary-bound, stomach awash with alcohol and pills;
messy on the rocks after the cliff-top leap;
lifeless in the car, engine running, pipe from exhaust

Get the message? Enough said!

Or rather, not enough said.
Might have been better if you'd said more.
Might have been better if you'd just
said how you feel . . .

THE ONE

She searched within for the big loyalty.
The big loyalty that would guide and hold
all her other loyalties.

creating
caring
making
family
duty
work
marriage
friends
leisure
shaping
money
travel
achieving
exploring
justice

All good in their way.
But she couldn't give everything equal weight.
There had to be a difficult sacrificing.

In those moments before death takes you,
what would you like to be able to say about your life?
What will your big loyalty have been?

YOU'RE "AVIN" A LAUGH!

The origin of a really good laugh
is the resurrection of Jesus.
The circus clown is hit across the head,
when his partner spins round holding that plank.
Another of Mr. Bean's schemes ends in humiliation.
The coyote loses again.
Tom finally traps Jerry
but is electrocuted by a loose wire.
We laugh.

Tragic, all of them.
But we laugh.

And we laugh because somewhere inside us,
we know that the loser will get up.
This is not the end of the story;
there's a future for them, for everyone.

Jesus said that where he went, we would go too.
In short, his resurrection was not a one-time thing.
It will be repeated.
Like a lot of TV comedy . . .

BACK TO BASICS

I want to be with you alone.
To walk the desert
for a thousand years.

I want to stand
on the edge of the planet with you.
Beside you,
inside you.
You're not afraid.
I'm not afraid.
In our different ways,
we've both been here before.

And then we step over the edge
and free fall together.
Free fall together
into God knows where . . .

And God does.

THE HOMECOMING

He felt like a stranger everywhere he went.
He'd walked and wandered
for so long.
He'd knocked on doors,
and slept on floors,
but all the time he'd wondered if he'd know;
if he'd know when he came home.
Tears welled in his eyes at the thought.
Imagine it.
Coming home.

Is it a place? A person? A feeling?
Where is home for you?
And can you go there?

FOUR THE FUTURE

It's New Year's Day, 1941, in the U.S.A.
The Economic Depression still hangs heavy.
The threat from Hitler is growing.

Hard times, as President Roosevelt
goes to his second-floor White House study,
to compose the speech that would launch
his unprecedented third term in office.

What words to speak?
There is a long silence.
Uncomfortably long.
His speech-writers wait.
And then he leans forward and begins dictating:

"We look forward to a world founded upon
four essential freedoms," he said.

"Freedom of expression.
Freedom of worship.
Freedom from want.
Freedom from fear."

There are a few things worth fighting for.

I WON'T REPEAT THIS

You'd think that after all these millennia,
it would no longer be true.
But it is.
God only makes originals.

Which means that people like you
don't come along very often.
Once, to be precise.

Out of nothing, something.
Out of nothing, life.
Out of nothing, you.

An original.
And your moment is now.

MIND THE GAP

God is nowhere.
God is now here.
Thin line, isn't it?